Christmas 1997
Karen –
Inspire all you meet!
Stephanie Mellon

The Golden Angel

Story and illustrations by
Stephanie Wellen

The Golden Angel

Story and illustrations by
Stephanie Wellen

Text copyright © 1995 by Stephanie Mellen

Illustrations copyright © 1995 by Stephanie Mellen

All rights reserved under International and Pan-American Copyright Conventions

Published in the United States

by Meltec Enterprises, 2978 Roundtree, Troy MI 48083-2346

The Golden Angel ™ is a trademark of Meltec Enterprises

Library of Congress Catalog Card Number: 94-79576

ISBN: 0-9637414-2-X

Manufactured in the United States of America

First Edition October 1995
10 9 8 7 6 5 4 3 2 1

Books written & illustrated by Stephanie Mellen

THE CRYSTAL RABBIT

A BEAR IN THE CHAIR

The Golden Angel

Books illustrated by Stephanie Mellen

THE TEENY TINY VOICE

Thank you *GOD* for taking care of me, may I continue to have the faith and courage to follow YOUR will . . .

To Marion Melvin and Sally George . . . thank you for touching my heart and encouraging me to give you this gift -- a *very* special gift . . .

Stephanie Mellen

The Golden Angel

It was the fifth
night of the blue
moon, month
unnamed, in a long
forgotten land.
Shimmering phantoms,
rising out of lost Soul-Memories,
silently fell across the stillness. Silvery purple mist
enveloped the sleepscape.

"Each person has a gift to give the world,
and, in that gift lies their destiny," quietly
whispered Elsbeth's Soul-Voice. Long forgotten
dreams. Long forgotten dreams.

It *was* impossible to escape the promise of
fulfillment yet to come . . .

How was it that
she finally chose
to come to this
time? This place?
So far, yet more
familiar than she cared to
remember. There was always some aspect of her
personality that was just out of reach.

Soft sleep eased her troubled mind. Peace swept through her SOUL.

Elsbeth longed for the secrets of those moments, irretrievably lost. To re-create -- yet, the knowledge eluded her. *Why*? The explanation seemed to slip through her grasp as easily as liquid moonbeams.

The Golden Angel

Night was the time she could no longer escape. "The Answer. *Where's* the answer?" pleaded Elsbeth's thoughts as she poured over the dusty gold leaf leather-bound tomes.

Searching. Listening to the words and the ideas of those long gone and those still present, some of whom she knew. THE Master Plan remained unknown until, piece by piece, it was given concrete form and joined with her Essence.

The Answer?

The Answer?

THE Answer . . .

Sleep gently embraced Elsbeth that night. Laying her head on the soft blue silk pillows, her Soul-Voice quietly whispered with a sense of determination and purpose, "Knowing. Knowing is all."

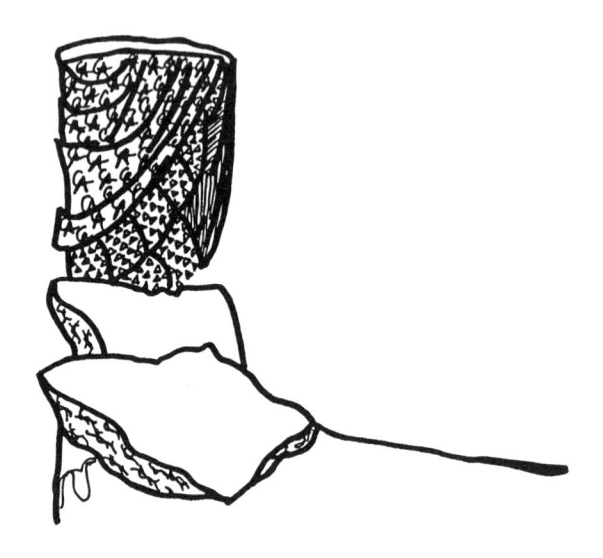

A warm, golden glow slowly filled her heart. Peace at last. How good it felt. The warmth held her gently, as the arms of a mother with a newborn child.

All in her SOUL's purpose-time . . .

The Golden Angel

The sweet, moist dampness of jasmine-scented dew brushed her cheek. Grudgingly, Elsbeth struggled to close her eyes.

"Knowing. Knowing is all. You cannot see the future by staring at the past. You **cannot** plan the future by the past."

*Our Life lessons are the **UNIVERSE**'s spiritual workout for the **SOUL** . . .*

Stephanie Mellen

Rain-splashed limestone chanted it's soothing lullaby in vain.

The Answer eluded her again, seemingly trapped forever in a labyrinth enigma. Torment filled the sleepscape that night, as it had so many nights before.

Why?

How?

WHEN?

The Golden Angel

The crimson red
glow of the candle
disclosed to
Elsbeth that it was
the morning side of
midnight. Grabbing the delicate
lavender silk down-filled covers,
she searched her dreams, re-listening to
muffled conversations heard in her mind-chamber,
for anything with 'The Answer'.

Too sleep-grogged to read. Her mind not quite awake. Yet, the torment -- the pain of the sleepscape -- would not allow her to return, at least for now.

Inside there was a restlessness . . .

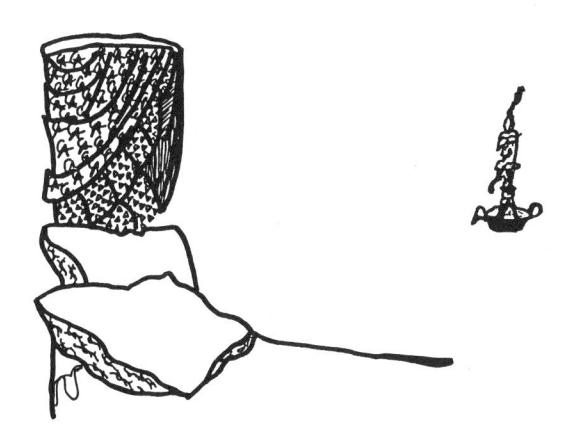

Stephanie Mellen

"I know The Answer. *I know I know* ! ! ! What *is* IT?"

"*Why* don't I remember? *Why*?"

"All in DIVINE right time. It *will* be revealed to you only when you are truly ready," gently whispered her Soul-Voice. "All in DIVINE right time."

It is not what you have been through -- it is what you are committed to . . .

"The Master Plan remains unknown until, piece by piece, it is given concrete form and grafted to your SOUL."

"The UNIVERSE has phrased and rephrased the structure of your Soul-Purpose until every minute action, each last nuance of your character, has contributed an integral component to your development."

Dream-cocooned, Elsbeth awakened to eye-opening Soul-Vision filled hours.

"Remain faithful to uncomplicated values. There is much more to mastery than blind faith in intuition. For intuition to mean anything, it has to be implemented. This requires a union of stringent perseverance and sheer hard work, backed by seasoned talents," her Soul-Voice divulged.

Reality now came more and more from the sleepscape's hidden caverns. **The** very caverns of her own SOUL. Those mist shrouded Soul-Memories which had been buried so deep. So long ago.

Feeling drowsy, no longer wanting to be of this place. This time. This world as she knew it.

"Where's the peace? The serenity? The promise?"

"*Where*? **Where**?"

Longing for a
softer, gentler
time, unknown by
those who have
passed before her,
and those who still are, the
creation of The Dream began to unfold, one
Soulbeat at a time. One Soulbeat at a time.

It *was* all happening perfectly. Magnificent concepts -- understanding them, developing them, and envisioning their successful completion . . .

Stephanie Mellen

It *was* the fifth night of the blue moon, month unnamed, in a long forgotten land.

One dreambeat at a time, elusive imprinted Soul-Memories awakened from her mind-chamber's recesses. Shaping and reshaping the structure of Elsbeth's SOUL, until every minute action, each last nuance contributed to her unfolding.

Remembrances of her destiny lay dormant, **but** *not* forgotten . . .

The Golden Angel

Beneath a lush canopy of trees, clinging ice-blue crystal dew drop diamonds glistened on the emerald green-bladed grass. Pristine burgundy flowers had appeared, intertwined with periwinkle bachelor buttons, nestled against a velvet-soft deep buttercup yellow backdrop.

Prickly brownish-black pine cones silently fell to their ephemeral earth blanket. New, spring green cones were forming.

The celebration of her SOUL renewal had begun ! ! !

Her Soul-Memory awakened.

Stephanie Mellen

"The same principles apply in the shaping and development of character. This has enabled our Soul-Memories to survive so well in our collective consciousness," disclosed The UNIVERSAL Voice.

"The SOUL depends on movement to achieve it's effect. Movement of **SPIRIT** -- a single image taken from one Life-frame will often seem static and lifeless. Fortunately, the last link in the elaborate UNIVERSAL chain includes character produced in various stages."

"Each Soul-Memory contains come clues to the secret of our purpose -- since each one is touched extensively by HIS influence. Explore the possibilities that are revealed by this Vision."

"May your SOUL's unfoldment be the seed of the idea, the dream, intermingled with Hope that will be a source of joy and inspiration to the WORLD."

Peace . . . Serenity . . .

The Golden Angel

"Peace is a gift of clarity. Learning. Healing. Grieving. Transformation unfolds when each lesson is mastered -- our SOULs timidly choosing to venture across the treacherous scaffolding in this temporary pool of Life."

"Just as clouds may fill the heavens to obscure the sun, so too does confusion temporarily mask the soft illumination of purpose -- revealed in it's own Soul-Time."

"Trust, My Child," gently whispered her Soul-Voice. "Trust."

Stephanie Mellen

    Unheard sounds of glistening ice-blue crystal diamond dew drops forming permeated the spring air. Emerald green blades of grass tenderly emerged, nudging aside their deep earth-brown blanket.

    Infinite numbers of cottonwood snow flakes drifted across the breeze's gentle surface -- gliding among the branches of overhanging trees until they vanished from sight through the open window of Elsbeth's bed chamber, guided by an invisible master puppeteer.

    The delicate lavender silk down-filled covers caressed her skin. Recollections of the innocent softness of a child's touch moved her heart.

    Elsbeth's Soul-Voice began to speak . . .

The Golden Angel

"My Child, no two roses on the bush open at the same time nor have the exact hue. So, too, do we each have our own unique Soul-Purpose -- unfolding, blossoming in perfect *UNIVERSAL*-time."

"Each spring green leaf seems undistinguishable from it's kin and neighbors. In time, their own Soul-Destiny unfolds -- a multitude of textured, shaded russet, orange, yellow, fiery red strata -- some, streaked with spring green."

"Each at the perfect moment -- it's own distinctive Soul-Voice has been awakened. Silently, slowly, gently to present a magnificent autumnal symphony."

Stephanie Mellen

"These Soul-Memories, abounding with color, fragrant scents, and distinct melodic images are part of *your* being, passing through your mind as I speak. Even thoughts of the tender young emerald green-bladed grass yet to be mown."

"Your SOUL, too, is as the seasons. At times gentle, even peace-filled on winter's coldest day. So too do the emerging Soul-Memories blend with **SPIRIT**."

"Have faith in your own abilities. I do."

"A world without light, without shadows, would be dark. Personal success does not come easily. Draw upon every available source of expertise. Your SOUL may mull over these impressions for years before it is permitted to attain the point of disclosure."

"Are you drawn to alter your person? Your speech? Your thoughts? Your adornments and possessions so that others will notice and approve?"

"Is the intent of this metamorphosis truly to realize your purpose?"

Stephanie Mellen

"The first may be accomplished in many ways. Through your own toil. As gifts from others. A crimp, a cut, a curl to your hair. Scents applied to your body. Adorning fine raiments."

"Yet, I pray, add to your own mind's tomes:

Am I happy only when I have these things?

Do I possess the precious gift of a kind smile? A gentle word for myself as well as others? Love-warmed thoughts of my life and those who have, are, and have yet to pass through?

Serenity? Peace? Gratitude for *all* which is in my life -- spiritually, emotionally, and physically?

Do I expect to come, in my heart and mind, as one day follows the other? From spring to winter? Birth to death?"

"These lessons are as a beautiful tapestry -- woven by our hidden awakening Soul-Memories."

The Golden Angel

                     Elsbeth's Soul-Self
                     listened cautiously.
                     Shadowesque
                     UNIVERSAL
                     memories faintly
               traced mauve-hazed
       images across her mind-screen --
Elsbeth seeing, for the first time, long ago
imprinted Soul-Visions -- *her* **DESTINY**.

Now her Soul-Self began to recognize and understand the UNIVERSAL whispers. Reverberating Soul-Memories bestowed ideas with the capacity of unprecedented lavishness. Munificent commodities.

What had once seemed but a dream was real. The torment and the pain now were fading into vast UNIVERSAL repositories.

Her Soul-agony soothed at last.

The Golden Angel

A warm golden glow first filled her heart. Then her body. Elsbeth's Soul-Voice tenderly lulled her to sleep. The deep healing sleep of a new born SOUL, freshly awakened, spiritually exhausted. *This* was **good** . . .

Now the mauve-hazed images paused. Lingering for brief eternity-seconds on her mind-screen -- as if to permanently invoke their Soul-connected messages.

Gentle words. Serene thoughts. Tranquil ideas. Soothing sounds. Comforting scents . . .

The Golden Angel

Ethereal UNIVERSAL whispers permeated her heart. "Sleep, My Child, sleep, for your Life has just begun. Your true Soul-Purpose soon will be revealed."

"Are the angels only of the Heavens? To be eluded. Nay. We *all* are angels."

"When we hug another do we not feel the sprout-stems, the base for our own angelic wings? Not shoulder blades - angelic sprout-stems for our Soul-Memories to be touched, stirred and awakened by others of our kind."

"You, My Child, are **THE GOLDEN ANGEL**. The UNIVERSE has chosen you to bring this message of Hope to this time-space called Earth."

"Is your hair of
golden color?
Your skin of
golden tones?
Nay. The gold of
the Soul-Spirit is more precious
and more valuable than *all* the treasures of *all* the
kingdoms of earth and sea."

"How many of us have wondered --

'Why am I here? What am I
supposed to do with my life?
Why is this happening to me
over and over again? I
don't want these lessons any
more!'

So many wounded Soul-Spirits have silently called
out loud, re-echoing screams of twisted pain."

"And, we escape by keeping busy, sleeping, feasting, living others Soul-Dreams. Why?"

"Once our Soul-Memories have been stirred, our Soul-Purpose will be revealed in DIVINE time."

Stephanie Mellen

"Temptations to Soul-slip are many --

    Just as a child stumbles with his first step . . .

    Just as we are encouraged to try another faltering stride, our own Soul-Voice encourages us not to give up Hope. Nor our dreams. Nor our lives."

The Golden Angel

"You, My Child,
are as I am today -
- you are now part
of what I always
was and who I always
will be . . ."

"May your words, thoughts, and actions be timeless. May the effects of your being continue into ETERNITY."

"Most of your life you have looked outside for THE ANSWER."

"Can you not see your physical body? Are not your feelings and your thoughts, too, a shrouded part of your being? Your memories?"

"Your identity, your SOUL has dimension. Even at this early date, grasping the concept -- immersed in every phase of it's creation."

"Upon realization of your Soul-Purpose you will still be in chaos. Before the decision of commitment is made, perhaps the most important resolution ever will be conceived. The genuine impact -- you *will* behold where the future abides."

"All of these we acknowledge. Yet, something more wonderful, more beautiful than you could ever imagine is unfolding. An essence contained in a delicate, unique form, pure in ***SPIRIT*** -- THE SOUL itself -- a beautiful golden, white light."

After decades of silence, THE MIRACLE appeared, prompted by circumstance and encouraged by temperament. Precisely timed. This was not the easiest of circumstances to achieve. The UNIVERSE had carefully affected every aspect of Elsbeth's SOUL.

The effect was unlike anything she had ever experienced before. Strongly reminiscent of elusive, yet embryonic, vivid memories.

The Golden Angel

"You, as we all, My Child, have a choice on this journey called LIFE -- to give, or to take."

- § **CHOOSE TO TAKE** -- your options vanish.

- § **CHOOSE TO GIVE**, from pure love and light, and the number of your options will be infinite.

- § **AS YOU MOVE TOWARD GREATER PEACE AND BALANCE**, you will experience eruption and shaking of your being. This is the cost of balance.

- § **THE MORE OUT OF BALANCE YOU ARE**, the more you will 'quake and mold'.

"Trust, My Child, your entire Essence will be brought into balance - slowly, steadily . . ."

"Tension may build. As you wish to change, there is also resistance once the 'quaking' of your SOUL occurs. Then a sense of freedom and inner peace."

"How can this bring balance?"

§ **THE GREATER THE LESSON**, so too will be the proportion of movement toward equilibrium. Thus, the stronger the effect.

§ **EXPLORE.** You have merely to comprehend one glimpse of your Soul-Purpose to remember specifically what to expect.

"The first brief look or two has no tangible direction. You possess the determination to initiate your Soul-Purpose *and* persist. Before long, you will have an invaluable role to render in the unfolding of others' Soul-Awakenings."

"Persevere. Continue to inspire all you meet. They, too, are seeking their purpose."

"Another personal crisis may strike. You may long to cease your journey. The loss of self, resulting directly from connection with your higher power - **GOD**, is essential for your Soul-renewal."

"To function at a higher level -- to achieve a sense of serenity, My Child,

- § **FIRST, trust *GOD* woven into the fabric of your life.**

    Sense the confidence. The warmth. The Power.

- § **THE SINGLE MOST SIGNIFICANT ATTRIBUTE IN YOUR *SOUL*'s FORMATION IS *FAITH*** -- preceded by Gratitude and Forgiveness."

Stephanie Mellen

REMEMBER**, one word captures the moment --* ***GOD. *The **SOUL** understands immediately.*

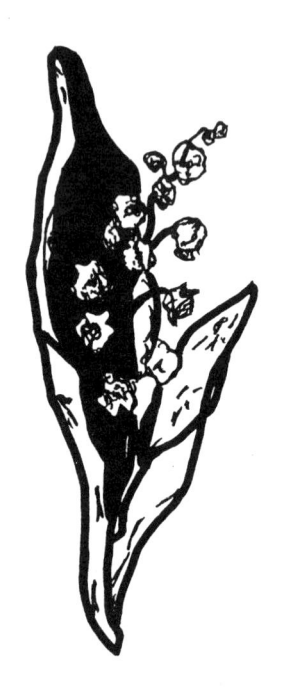

"It would seem that **GOD**, at the beginning, thought of these Soul-Memories as little more than a novelty that might help promote this UNIVERSAL system. The power of successes past has proven that Soul-renewal is essential."

*BEGIN your Soul-Journey and
the* **LORD** *will guide you.*

"Never underestimate the importance of fear, for without it true humility and willingness cannot unveil the course for your SOUL's emergence."

*Forgiveness is the willingness to
surrender our attempt to change
the past.*

"There will be day-spans you appear to be insignificant -- without purpose. Trust. Eventually the plan is revealed."

§ **FEEL the *SPIRIT*** -- senses stirred. Minds eased. Listen. Just listen . . .

"Losses may be serious, coming quickly -- DO NOT break stride. Use your Soul-Memories to experience, to continue, this Life adventure. **GOD** is your faithful companion."

"Enjoy. Your fears will become less significant, and, eventually vanish."

"Others who have also had their Soul-Purpose revealed will come together. Sharing their experiences as stories -- their prowess honed in this theater called Life."

§ **GIVE THE GIFT OF SERVICE.** Being ***GOD*** inspired is a world unto itself.

A Presence now. A future that will appreciate in decades to come.

§ GET in touch with *SPIRIT* . . .

You have already got the power, and then,

only then, will you receive an *exciting gift.*

The triumph of SPIRIT.

The source of enchantment. A gift. An extraordinary gift . . .

"Pray daily. **GOD** already knows whose lives you are meant to touch. Once your Soul-Purpose is revealed, have the Faith and the Courage to follow **GOD**'s will. Attain the experience necessary to achieve your dreams, perhaps in a somewhat different manner than that which has been established."

Not one experience has been wasted.
Know, apart from anything else, you
fit perfectly with the UNIVERSE.
We each have an important purpose -
our own unique DESTINY.

"These Life Lessons are interesting, unlike any other. All has been planned by **GOD**, *the* most competent draftsman - imprinted in our Soul-Memories."

The Golden Angel

§ **SHOW YOUR HONESTY, INTEGRITY, AND PERSONAL CARING.** These My Child, are the gentle winds of change.

Knowing. Knowing is all. Your heart remembers even when you do not.

§ **BE WISE.** Lightness of being and spiritual understatement restore Hope.

"When changes seemingly occur at random, know they are meant to inspire. It is the ideal system for molding our SOUL. This enables us to participate even more closely, allowing us to ascertain at a glance precisely what needs to be accomplished on our part."

*SURRENDER your will to **GOD**, so it may be enhanced, if so deemed.*

"You might feel driven or barely broken. A disturbance of your SOUL may occur. This is part of the plan to elevate you to a higher level of Spiritually."

"Once initiated, use your awareness diligently, with pure intentions. Be assured you are on target. Then you will see the advantages."

§ **SERENITY.** It just feels right.

Nothing appears in our lives that does not contribute either to the development of our character or the revelation of our true Purpose.

"Crammed into this framework of Life is a profusion of Soul-Visions -- details that are almost overwhelming -- compressed into one lifetime."

Nothing need be left to chance and nothing is. The UNIVERSE is never late.

"The old self may never be destroyed. It lingers as a faint remembrance. Celebrate your Spiritual growth, as well as whatever frailties and strengths. You are being molded and shaped intentionally. Experience your true potential, which is unlike anything previously imagined."

§ **AND** what does it to be the best? The balance of forces.

Spiritual. Emotional. Physical.

*Master the art of prayer and meditation. Spend time with **GOD**.*

"From inception, this association at first established in your dreamscape, will manifest gifts of DIVINE inspiration."

"Spend time forming visible ideas for the future, improvise on existing themes, to trigger the imagination and the Soul-Memories of others. Reflect and express Gratitude for **GOD**'s influence -- imbued in **SPIRIT**."

"As you continue to evolve, **GOD**'s influence will be felt, along with greater clarity. Once you discover your Soul-Purpose, barriers will dissolve into a pool of lost limitations. Make your Soul-Purpose known Universally."

> "Remember, My Child, say IT without saying a word."

"First, retreat to serenity. Then, commitment, dedication, excellence. You *are* a beacon of help, hope, and encouragement for those in need."

Your Soul-Journey is on target.

Every wish,

every dream,

every desire is achievable ! ! !

"Subtle changes will occur, almost imperceptible. To follow these principles is not easy. As your skills are perfected and expanded, you will reveal yourself to others who also have been drawn to their own transformation."

"Your own unique metamorphosis is filled with possibilities. Thus, your abilities will enable you to achieve more than before."

"This is a time created to enjoy, renew, remember, discover the *real* you. The you you never knew. The you you always dreamed of. *You* have discovered your mission."

DARE TO BE MORE. You are the creation of a UNIVERSAL dream.

"There is a change coming and it is exciting. A subtle **SPIRIT**-filled positive energy."

This week.

Next week.

Every week!

§   **BE GENEROUS WITH YOUR TALENT.** The art of being true to your Soul-Self is knowing when to be willing, humble, and grateful. *NEVER* settle for less.

"A once in a lifetime adventure awaits you. YOU ARE NEVER ALONE. **FOCUS.** You have never felt like this before."

The Golden Angel

§ **YOU are a new, beautiful, loving Soul-Spirit which is emerging.** The renewing power of **GOD** is the single source to everything you need.

It is *your* experience. A personal experience . . .

and, *you are closer than you realize*!

§ **YOU have been given so much.** May you touch and inspire the hearts and the Soul-Memories of *all* you meet.

*REMEMBER, with **GOD** there is no limit to how far you can go.*

*The difficult **GOD** does automatically. The impossible takes a few seconds more.*

Stephanie Mellen

"My Child," gently whispered **THE** Soul-Voice of the UNIVERSE. "Go forth, you *are* ***THE GOLDEN ANGEL***."

And, so, it was written . . .

The Golden Angel